TRICKED BY THE KIDS
CRONUS THE TITAN TELLS ALL

by Eric Braun

illustrated by Stephen Gilpin

A WIFE'S BETRAYAL!

A FATHER'S WARNING!

CRONUS IN PAIN: "For the love of Sky, my belly hurts!"

PICTURE WINDOW BOOKS
a capstone imprint

In the earliest Greek mythology, Titans and Giants roamed the world. They were the children of the Sky and the Earth, and they were monsters. The most dangerous of the Titans was Cronus. He ruled the world. But the Sky said that Cronus' children would overthrow him one day. To protect himself, Cronus swallowed his children as soon as they were born. His wife, who hated to see her children disappear, hid the sixth child, Zeus. When Zeus grew up, he freed his brothers and sisters from inside their father. Together they began a war with Cronus and the Titans that lasted 10 years. When Zeus and his siblings won the war, they ruled the world from Mount Olympus— and Cronus and the other Titans were sent to prison in Tartarus, the underworld.

That's the classic version of the story.

But how would Cronus tell it?

Everyone has heard of the great gods and goddesses of Olympus. They were good-looking and powerful. And they saved the world from the awful monsters that came before them.

You're looking at one of the "awful monsters."

If you knew the truth, though, you wouldn't think I was so awful. When I ruled the world, it was peaceful. Nobody fought, argued, or even raised a voice. It was such a good time that everyone called it the Golden Age.

Then things fell apart.

3

My father, the Sky, liked to be in control of everything. He had trouble just sitting back, enjoying life, and letting me run the show. So, in the midst of our Golden Age, he locked everyone up inside the Earth, including the Titans, Cyclopes, and Giants.

But I wasn't going to let my dad treat everyone that way. So I cut him with a sickle. That taught him a lesson!

"Someday your children will fight against you," he warned, "just like you fought me. They will defeat you and rule the world."

At first I didn't worry too much about what my dad said. I freed my brothers and sisters, and things were good again. We enjoyed all the things Titans and Giants enjoy: gold, music, and big dinners. We even lived peacefully with humans. Imagine that!

My wife, Rhea, and I were especially happy. I loved
her very much and treated her like a queen. When
Rhea became pregnant with our first child, I was as
happy as any father would be.

But then I started to worry. What if my dad was right? After all, he was the Sky—and very wise. Maybe my children were destined to rise up against me.

I looked around at all the happy Titans and Giants. Things were going really well. Who knew what kind of rulers my children would be? If they were mean enough to start a war, they would be mean rulers too.

Once again I made a decision to protect everyone.

When Rhea gave birth to our first child, Hestia, I did what had to be done. I grabbed that baby and swallowed her whole.

I know, I know. You probably think it's gross and terrible. Maybe this is why the stories call me a "monster." But think of it this way: I gave up my own child to help protect everyone else. I didn't want to do it, but I had to do it to be a good ruler.

When my next four children were born, I swallowed them too. First I swallowed Demeter, then Hera, Hades, and Poseidon.

They were big and solid, and they dropped like big stones inside of me.

BURP

My last child was Zeus. Rhea begged me not to swallow him. She really wanted us to raise this boy together as normal parents. But I had a duty to fulfill. So into my belly he went. Like his brothers and sisters, he dropped like a stone.

Things were OK for a while after that. My kids, the Olympians, were in my belly, and I didn't worry about war breaking out. Life was good.

One day, Rhea invited a stranger over to our house for tea. He offered me a drink with some special herbs in it. We often had parties and guests, so I had no reason not to trust this man.

I drank it.

Right away I felt like my insides twisted upside down. An explosion went off in my stomach. A moment later I was burping up my children: one, two, three, four, five, six! And they were all grown up!

THUNK

Actually, I burped up *five* of my kids ... and a stone.

There was a lot of yelling after that. My stomach felt awful, and I hollered in pain. The Olympians must have thought I was threatening them, because they started yelling too.

They yelled things like, "This is war!" and "You should never swallow children!" They also yelled, "Kill Cronus!" Me! Their dad!

Here's the scoop: Rhea had tricked me. My own dear wife! I never swallowed Zeus. Rhea hid him with some nymphs in Crete. She wrapped up a stone in baby clothes, told me it was Zeus, and I swallowed it. I guess she had grown tired of me storing all our children in my belly.

coo

The stranger with the tea, then, was Zeus. He had
teamed up with Rhea to trick me. I tell you, if you
can't trust the love of your life, whom can you trust?

My heart was broken, and I took out my despair on
the battlefield. I fought fiercely.

The Cyclopes betrayed us and joined the Olympians. They made thunderbolts for Zeus to throw at us. They made a helmet of invisibility that Hades wore to sneak up on us. And they made a trident for Poseidon. The weapon was so powerful, he used it to make storms in the sea that sent huge waves ashore and drowned many of us Titans.

Swords clashed. We kicked up mountains, splashed water out of lakes, and tore up forests by the roots.

After 10 years it was over. The Olympians had defeated us. They imprisoned us Titans in a dark, gloomy pit under the earth called Tartarus. Then they divided up the universe, and Zeus became the ruler of everything, sitting high atop Mount Olympus.

It all happened just like my
father said it would.

So here I sit in Tartarus, along with my Titan brothers and sisters.

All the stories make the Olympians look good and the Titans look like monsters. But let me ask you this: Was there ever another Golden Age? No.

And should you ever drink tea from a stranger?

DEFINITELY NOT.

Critical Thinking Using the Common Core ★ ★ ★ ★ ★ ★

This version of the classic Greek myth "War of the Titans" is told by Cronus the Titan, from his point of view. If Rhea told the story, what details might she tell differently? What if Zeus told the story from his point of view? (Integration of Knowledge and Ideas)

Explain why Cronus thought it was a good idea to swallow his six children. (Key Ideas and Details)

Describe the steps Rhea took to trick Cronus, first when their son Zeus was a baby, and then when Zeus was a grown man. (Craft and Structure)

Glossary ★ ★ ★ ★ ★ ★ ★ ★ ★ ★ ★ ★ ★ ★ ★ ★ ★ ★ ★

Cyclops—a one-eyed giant

defeat—to beat someone in a competition

destined—foretold to happen

mythology—old or ancient stories told again and again that help connect people with their past

Olympus—the highest mountain in Greece, and in Greek mythology the home of the Greek gods

point of view—a way of looking at something

sickle—a tool with a curved blade and short handle, usually used in farming

Tartarus—a mythical underground pit used as a prison

trident—a spear with three tips; the weapon of Poseidon

version—an account of something from a certain point of view

Read More

Bryant, Megan E. *Oh My Gods!: A Look-It-Up Guide to the Gods of Mythology.* Mythlopedia. New York: Scholastic: Franklin Watts, 2010.

Meister, Cari. *The Battle of the Olympians and the Titans: a Retelling.* Mankato, Minn.: Picture Window Books, 2012.

O'Connor, George. *Zeus: King of the Gods.* Olympians. New York: London: First Second, 2010.

Internet Sites

FactHound offers a safe, fun way to find Internet sites related to this book. All of the sites on FactHound have been researched by our staff.

Here's all you do:

Visit *www.facthound.com*

Type in this code: 9781479521845

Super-cool stuff! Check out projects, games and lots more at **www.capstonekids.com**

Thanks to our advisers for their expertise, research, and advice:

Susan C. Shelmerdine, PhD, Professor of Classical Studies
University of North Carolina, Greensboro

Terry Flaherty, PhD, Professor of English
Minnesota State University, Mankato

Editor: Jill Kalz
Designer: Lori Bye
Art Director: Nathan Gassman
Production Specialist: Kathy McColley
The illustrations in this book were created digitally.

Picture Window Books are published by Capstone,
1710 Roe Crest Drive, North Mankato, Minnesota 56003
www.capstonepub.com

Library of Congress Cataloging-in-Publication Data
Braun, Eric, 1971–
  Cronus the titan tells all : tricked by the kids / by Eric Braun, illustrated by
Stephen Gilpin.
    pages cm. — (Nonfiction picture books. The other side of the myth.)
  Summary: "Introduces the concept of point of view through Cronus' retelling of
the classic Greek myth 'War of the Titans'"—Provided by publisher.
  ISBN 978-1-4795-2184-5 (library binding)
  ISBN 978-1-4795-2941-4 (paperback)
  ISBN 978-1-4795-3320-6 (eBook PDF)
1. Cronus (Greek deity)—Juvenile literature. I. Gilpin, Stephen illustrator II. Title.
  BL820.C64B73 2014
  398.20938'01—dc23   2013046715

photo credit: Jefferson Wheeler

About the Author

Eric Braun writes fiction and nonfiction for kids,
teens, and adults, but sometimes he dreams
of being a professional skateboarder. He is a
McKnight Fellow and also a nice fellow. He lives
in Minneapolis with his wife, sons, and gecko.

Look for all the books in the series:

Printed in the United States of America in North Mankato, Minnesota.
032014   008087CGF14